working
in teams

ALISON HARDINGHAM

Alison Hardingham read Experimental Psychology at Oxford University. After graduating she joined the education service as a psychologist, providing services for emotionally disturbed children, their teachers and their families. A major career move in the mid-1980s took her into consultancy and she is currently a director of Interactive Skills Limited, a human resource consultancy specialising in assessment, management development and organisation development. She has written many books on psychology, personal effectiveness, and HR issues. She is the author *Designing Training* (1996), *Psychology for Trainers* (1998) and, with Charlotte Ellis, *Exercises for Team Development* (1999), all published by the CIPD.

Management Shapers is a comprehensive series covering all the crucial management skill areas. Each book includes the key issues, helpful starting points and practical advice in a concise and lively style. Together, they form an accessible library reflecting current best practice – ideal for study or quick reference.

The Chartered Institute of Personnel and Development is the leading publisher of books and reports for personnel and training professionals, students, and all those concerned with the effective management and development of people at work. For full details of all our titles, please contact the Publishing Department:

tel. 020-8263 3387
fax 020-8263 3850
e-mail publish@cipd.co.uk

The catalogue of all CIPD titles can be viewed on the CIPD website:
www.cipd.co.uk/publications

working
in teams

ALISON HARDINGHAM

Chartered Institute of Personnel and Development

First published in the *Training Extras* series in 1995
Reprinted 1997
First published in the *Management Shapers* series in 1998
Reprinted 2000

Design by Curve
Typesetting by Paperweight
Printed in Great Britain by
The Guernsey Press, Channel Islands

British Library Cataloguing in Publication Data
A catalogue record for this book is available from the
British Library

ISBN
0-85292-767-3

The views expressed in this book are the author's own and
may not necessarily reflect those of the CIPD.

Chartered Institute of Personnel and Development, CIPD House,
Camp Road, London SW19 4UX
Tel.: 020 8971 9000   Fax: 020 8263 3333
E-mail: cipd@cipd.co.uk   Website: www.cipd.co.uk
Incorporated by Royal Charter. Registered charity no. 1079797

contents

Other titles in the series:

introduction

This book has been written for people who are in teams, and who want to make sure their teams work as well as possible.

Some or all of the following may apply to you:

- you may be about to join a new team

- you may be leading a team for the first time

- you may be about to attend or have just attended a teambuilding programme

- you may be an experienced team member or team leader who wants to check out the latest thinking on teams.

This book is designed to help, with easy-to-read information, examples from teams in different kinds of organisations, and quizzes and questionnaires to get you thinking. The theory is there because it is relevant to effective teamworking, and it is presented in a way that, hopefully, allows you to relate it to your own experiences.

That is why questions and answers are used extensively throughout. You may find you get most out of the text by thinking how you would answer the questions before reading the answers supplied! In any event, you will be pleased to know that the questions around which the book is structured are the very ones that the team leaders and team members I work with ask most frequently. So I hope you will find they address the things about teamworking that most interest, frustrate or intrigue you.

1 what makes a group of people a team?

What's the difference between a 'team' and a 'group'?

I often come across people who are confused about whether they are in a 'real' team or not. They look at classic teams (in football, the military and music, for example) and they see little in common with their own 'team' at work. So they often conclude that they are not a 'real' team, and that the lessons and experiences of teams are not relevant to them.

In fact, there is one key question you need to ask yourself when you're trying to decide whether your work group is a team or not. That question is: *Do all the members of my group share at least one goal that can be accomplished only through the joint efforts of us all?*

Think of a group you belong to at work. Is there a shared goal? Do you all need to work together to achieve it? If the answer is 'yes', that group is a team.

The shared goal or goals are the difference between a team and a group. So in any organisation there are many teams and many groups, and most of us belong to several of each at any one time. You may for example be part of a group of people that share the same office, a group that takes their lunchbreak together, and a group that is available for certain types of overtime. You may also belong to a project team, and a specialist team supplying particular skills to the organisation.

The special requirements, benefits and risks of teams come into play as soon as there is at least one shared goal that demands joint efforts. This is because the goal or goals need to be understood in the same way by all the team members and the joint efforts need to be co-ordinated. So the risks inherent in high levels of interaction and communication rise, as do the possible pay-offs from successful co-operation and collaboration.

Why do teams need special attention?

When a team doesn't get the help it needs to protect itself against the risks of teamworking, and to deliver the pay-offs, all sorts of problems arise. They range from uncomfortable and destructive meetings to individuals in the team feeling hurt or demotivated.

If you think about the difference between a football team and a team at work, it's easy to see why such problems arise as often as they do. In the table opposite I've listed just a few of these differences.

Comparing a football team with a typical work team

Football team:	Work team:
◎ clearly defined role for everyone in the team	◎ many people not sure where they or others fit
◻ concrete, measurable goal	◻ often the goal(s) of the team have never been spelled out – different people have different ideas of what they are!
△ visible competition for the team to unite against	
◎ has a coach	△ as much competition inside the team as outside it
	◎ is left to its own devices

In the next chapter I shall look in more detail at some of the most common problems that arise in work teams and at the special attention that can be given to our teams at work to prevent or cure them. Here, I simply want to point out that really successful teams are successful because of a great deal of effort and structure. Yet at work we often expect groups of people to turn themselves into teams instantly and without help.

What is meant by the 'team life-cycle'?

As well as understanding the difference between a team and a group, it's useful to understand the different stages that teams go through as they work together. It helps us again to recognise teams at work, and see what all teams have in common even when they look very different.

As soon as a group of people has one or more shared goals it starts organising itself to achieve them. But it can't start work immediately. Certain basics of human interaction have to be taken care of first, and research has shown there is a set of fairly predictable stages. This set of stages is known as the 'team life-cycle'. A summary of the stages and how to recognise them is represented in the table opposite.

When is a team a 'superteam'?

There has been a great deal of research recently into what makes an exceptional team. And members of teams often hope that theirs is or can be a 'superteam' or a 'high-performing team'. After all, it takes a lot of effort to build and belong to a team. It's not surprising we all hope our teams are something special. The bullet list below gives the key characteristics of 'superteams', according to the research. A 'superteam' is defined by:

- effective and enjoyable communication between team members

- a very effective team-working approach, which all members are skilled in using

- commitment on the part of team members to one another's personal growth and success, as well as to achievement of the goals

The team life-cycle

Stage 1:	team is:	signs may include:
	◉ 'undeveloped'	◉ self-conscious politeness
	▣ 'forming'	▣ embarrassment
	△ concerned with 'who fits where'	△ enthusiasm
		◉ stilted communication
		◉ 'honeymoon' feelings
		◉ not much achieved work-wise
Stage 2:	team is:	signs may include:
	◉ 'experimenting'	◉ conflict
	▣ 'storming'	▣ lively debate and discussion
	△ concerned with 'how we work together'	△ trying out ways of working as a team
		◉ things beginning to be achieved
Stage 3:	team is:	signs may include:
	◉ 'mature'	◉ relaxed, purposeful atmosphere
	▣ 'performing'	▣ feelings of confidence
	△ concerned with achieving the goals	△ most talk being about the job
		◉ goals being achieved!
Stage 4:	team is:	signs may include:
	◉ 'ending'	◉ tying up loose ends
	▣ 'mourning'	▣ celebrating achievement
	△ concerned with breaking up and moving on to new tasks	△ feelings of sadness
		◉ planning for new teams
		◉ saying goodbyes

- processes for and success in continuous improvement of its own methods and outputs

- high levels of creativity

- ability to deal with the most difficult, subtle, and conflict-provoking issues.

However, just as important as being able to recognise a superteam is being able to recognise when you don't need one, or need to be in one. An effective team is a team that achieves its purpose. Many purposes do not require superteams. Building a superteam is in that case at best an irrelevant luxury, at worst a recipe for disillusionment.

What kind of team do I belong to?

Hopefully, you can already recognise whether you belong to a team at work and, if so, what stage of development it is at, and whether or not it is a 'superteam'. There are some further questions you might find it useful to ask yourself about your team as a step towards deciding how effectively it is achieving its goals, and what particular obstacles and opportunities there are for it. These questions are listed in the table opposite.

One of the biggest challenges for people who want to make teams work in organisations is the sheer complexity of such teams and their interrelationships. The questions in the table opposite will help you begin to take account of this complexity.

Understanding your team

Whom, if anyone, is my team meant to beat?

- Will my team be competing against other teams?
- Are those competing teams inside or outside the organisation?
- What are the benefits of competition?
- What are the disadvantages?
- Is there a risk of my team competing inappropriately?
- On balance, is it more important for my team to compete and win successfully or to co-operate with other teams?

Do we need clearly defined roles in my team?

- To what extent does the achievement of team goals depend on two or more members working closely together?
- To what extent do the interactions, information exchange and joint working of team members need to be orderly, predictable, and polished? If they are casual, will my team still succeed?
- Could any team member fulfil any of the roles, or are there a large number of 'specialist' roles?
- Do you envisage team members swapping roles?

How close a 'family' is my team?

- How important is loyalty to the team?
- What are the disadvantages of loyalty?
- Are team size and team membership fixed?
- To what extent do people need to belong to more than one team?
- What proportion of team members will be part-time?
- What will be the pattern of contribution of the 'part-timers'?
- Is there any benefit in the team involving 'guests' and 'visitors'?
- Is there a risk of performance suffering if others know what's going on inside this team? Does the activity need to be 'secret'?
- Are people too ready, or not ready enough, to join in other teams' activities?
- How long are people likely to remain members of the team?
- What are the advantages of people staying in one team for long periods?
- What are the disadvantages?

How happy am I with my team?

If you have been thinking about what kind of team you belong to and what it's meant to achieve, you are probably already asking yourself whether it's up to the job. Whether you're a team leader or just a team-member, your feelings about your team will be an invaluable barometer of how well it's functioning.

● Do you feel proud to belong to this team?

■ Do you enjoy team meetings?

▲ Are you confident in the team's ability to achieve?

If the answer to any of these questions is 'no', you might like to embark on some further diagnosis of what could be wrong. The table below gives you a framework for diagnosis.

A framework for diagnosing what's wrong with a team

Questions about objectives

- ○ Why was this team formed?
- ▫ What does it do?
- △ What is its overall purpose?
- ○ What are its critical success factors?
- ○ What are its priorities?
- ○ What external information does it need to respond to?
- ▫ What should change as a result of this team's work?
- △ What is the best that this team could achieve?
- ○ What bad consequences will ensue if this team fails?
- ○ How might this team contribute to the organisation's success?
- ○ How might this team contribute to the organisation's failure?

Questions about achievement

- Overall, how well would you say the team was doing against its objectives?
- Why would you say that?
- What does it need to improve?
- Will it achieve all its objectives in time?
- Which objective will it achieve best? Why?
- Which objective is it most likely to fail? Why?
- Is it likely to achieve more than it set out to? In what way? Why?
- What might happen within the team in the future to prevent achievement?
- What external conditions might the team face that would prevent or threaten achievement?
- Will the team be able to overcome those sorts of difficulties and still achieve? Why/why not?
- What pleases you most about the team's level of achievement?
- What (if anything) would need to change for you to be absolutely confident that the team will achieve?

Questions about feelings

- On balance, do you enjoy working in this team?
- What do you like about it?
- What do you dislike about it?
- What would need to change for you to like it more?
- When do you feel most annoyed or upset?
- When do you feel most pleased or happy?
- Have your feelings changed over the time the team has been in operation? How?
- Would you like to leave this team? Why/why not?
- Are there other team members you particularly like working with? Why?
- Are there other team members you particularly dislike working with? Why?
- Do you feel valued as a team member? Why/why not?
- Are there any things about working in this team that cause you stress? What are they?

If you want a quick mental check-list for making on-the-spot appraisals of team functioning, try the following acronym: PERFORM. It stands for:

Productivity: is the team getting enough done?

Empathy: do the team members feel comfortable with one another?

Roles & goals: do they know what they're supposed to be doing?

Flexibility: are they open to outside influence and contribution?

Openness: do they say what they think?

Recognition: do they praise one another and publicise achievement?

Morale: do people want to be in this team?

And the most common indicators of problems in any of these areas are:

Productivity: a boss in a bad temper

Empathy: no coffee at team meetings

Roles & goals: puzzled faces

Flexibility: annoyed outsiders talking about the 'fortress mentality'

Openness: silence

Recognition: backbiting

Morale: everyone has left!

What are the advantages and disadvantages of teams at work?

By now you may be thinking that with all the risks and pitfalls it might be better to avoid teams at work – that it might be better to package the work up so that *individuals* are responsible for discrete packages, so avoiding the need for truly joint working. So let's take a cool look at the advantages and disadvantages for organisations of teams at work. If the 'cons' are outweighing the 'pros' for any team that you know of or belong to, it may be time to think about organising the work differently.

The main, and most common, disadvantages to teamworking are these:

- Too much time and energy are spent improving communication and interactive skills. Work suffers as a consequence.

- Particular individuals are embarrassed or marginalised because they find teamworking difficult, and contrary to their natural style. (I have met people who are actually frightened at the prospect of having to work in teams!)

- Teams start competing with one another, to the detriment of the organisation as a whole.

These disadvantages are so serious in their potential effects that teamworking needs to be a deliberate choice, not an accident. The main advantages which may lead an

organisation to make the choice for teams are listed below –
and, when they are realised in practice, they can transform
morale and profitability.

● Working in teams can release creativity and energy.
Communication in effective teams is genuinely
interactive, with people building on one another's
suggestions, adding fresh perspectives which move the
discussion forward, and showing interest in others'
comments on their own points.

■ Working in teams can mean people enjoy work more.
We all like, and need, to belong. Working in teams
satisfies that basic human need.

▲ Working in teams can lead to improvements in efficiency.
When people are planning and implementing a variety
of activities together, with ongoing co-operation and
constant communication, they are able to identify many
ways to improve how the work is organised, how
information, ideas, and outputs flow, and how different
activities influence one another's critical paths. This is
one of the main reasons why so many organisations
seeking to reduce costs and improve productivity have
introduced teamworking.

● Sometimes teamworking is the only way to do a job. This
is not strictly an 'advantage'. But in all this discussion
of when and whether to choose teamworking, we mustn't
forget that sometimes there is no choice. Neither a
concert nor a play can be performed without teamwork.

And neither can many essential and mundane organisational tasks.

The rest of this book is concerned with how to make teams work – because both by choice and by necessity they are, and will continue to be, key to organisational life.

2 what can go wrong with teams?

All kinds of things can go wrong with teams. In this chapter I shall describe eight problems common to teams, and what you can do to find solutions.

Problem No. 1: meetings, bloody meetings

For many people with whom I have talked about teamworking, 'teamwork' equals 'meetings'. This is particularly true when meetings go badly. There are many symptoms of meetings that wreck, rather than build, teams:

- People turn up late.

- Meetings overrun.

- Meetings are boring.

- People don't contribute much to discussion.

- The first item on the agenda takes for ever, so all the subsequent items have to be rushed through.

- People leave feeling frustrated, angry, exhausted, or depressed.

- People who should be there don't turn up (excuses are imaginative!).

▲ One or two people dominate the whole meeting.

◉ Meetings are used as a forum for settling private scores.

◉ Decisions are either not made or are arbitrarily imposed by the team leader after inconclusive discussion.

If all or any of these symptoms apply to meetings between members of your team, you will recognise how destructive such meetings are. Because meetings are where the whole team gets together, their influence on team functioning and team spirit is profound. Not only are bad meetings a lost opportunity to realise some of the biggest benefits of teamworking, they are also a place where the human relationships on which effective teamworking depends can be irretrievably damaged. So what can be done about the 'meetings, bloody meetings' problem?

It is surprising how much can be achieved by the introduction of straightforward 'meetings discipline':

◉ Agenda and papers are circulated well in advance.

▣ Meetings start and finish on time.

▲ Good chairmanship is exercised.

◉ Clear action points are made, to be reviewed at the next meeting.

◉ Minutes are circulated within two days of the meeting.

● A 10-minute review of the meeting's effectiveness is held before the close.

If this isn't enough, two further routes are worth pursuing. One is to introduce a structured, group problem-solving process so that team decision-making is both more effective and more enjoyable. (Details of such a process can be found on pages 53–55.) The second is to ask someone from outside the team to provide some 'process consultancy' to a meeting, or a series of meetings. The key elements of 'process consultancy' are:

● the use of someone who is not part of the team to observe and comment on the team at work

■ setting aside time to review 'process issues' – that is, issues to do with *how* the team works.

If you would like to know more about process consultancy and how it might help your team, you will find more facts (and examples) in *Pulling Together: Teamwork in practice* by the present author and Jenny Royal (1994, IPD).

Problem No. 2: sloping shoulders

Sometimes teams suffer from the reverse of Problem No. 1. Their meetings are fast-moving, highly participative, and fun. They generate huge numbers of ideas, and decisions are made through a truly group process on a range of issues. But nothing happens between meetings. No one delivers. Sloping shoulders are everywhere, under the cloak of 'team responsibility'.

The temptation for the team leader and the more diligent members of the team is to start blaming other people when this problem arises. The idea is that the more severely individuals are punished for failing to deliver in the past, the more likely they are to deliver in the future.

In my experience this 'solution' has only a short-term positive effect on delivery, and a long-term negative effect on teamworking. Individuals start seeking to avoid taking responsibility in the first place, participation and creativity drop, and an atmosphere of mutual recrimination sets in.

A better approach is to address the fundamental question of individual commitment to team objectives. The table opposite suggests a way of doing this. (It is often useful to have an outside facilitator to help teams through this process.)

You can also straighten sloping shoulders by:

- making sure every action decided by the team has an individual's name attached to it

- checking the named individual has understood and agreed to the action

- reviewing the progress of all actions at the next meeting

Structure for taking a team through the objective-setting process

Question addressed	Activity	Output
What are the critical success factors for our organisation at this point in time?	Team discussion, possibly with initial presentation of factual information on eg market and financial position or company business plan by team leader or 'outsider'.	Summary of critical success factors for the organisation; understanding and acceptance of those by the team.
↓		
Where can our team best contribute to achieving them? What are the priorities for the team?	Team discussion, possibly with initial presentation of team leader's thoughts and reasons for them.	Summary of team's objectives and critical success factors, contributed to and accepted by whole team.
↓		
What can each team member best contribute to achieving the team objectives?	Individual reflection or discussion in pairs or small groups; followed by presentation back to whole group by each individual for comment.	Draft set of objectives for each team member, understood, contributed to, and committed to, by whole team.
↓		
If each of us meets our objectives, will our team have made a significant contribution to the success of the organisation?	Team discussion.	Motivation.

- exploring, where they haven't been completed, the reason why (in a helpful, not a blaming, way) and checking what other team members can do in support

- remembering to publicise and celebrate achievements.

It's important to keep to these simple disciplines even when 'sloping shoulders' are not a big problem for your team. They help to prevent people sliding away from being a real work team that gets things done towards being simply an unstructured group that has fun together. And prevention is better than cure.

Problem No. 3: between-team rivalry

Between-team rivalry is only a problem if it damages the organisation as a whole. Sometimes it's a benefit, as when fiercely competing sales teams drive the overall sales up and up, or mildly competing 'improvement groups' implement initiative after initiative to cut costs.

The symptoms of problematic between-team rivalry are these:

- Work isn't done: one team blames another.

- Information flow between teams is erratic or slow even though the information is important.

▲ When one team asks for help from another the answer is 'It's your problem.'

● Tasks requiring co-operation between teams run into serious difficulties, regularly.

● People strongly dislike transferring from one team to another.

Two sorts of initiatives help overcome inappropriate between-team rivalry. The first is initiatives that bring all, or parts, of teams together. These include:

● social events

■ teambuilding activities where real work teams are 'mixed up'

▲ inviting members of other teams to attend your meetings

● identifying problems shared between you and other teams, and setting up mixed-team task groups to solve them.

The second sort of helpful initiative is introducing ways to measure team effectiveness that include looking at how well one team provides a service to fellow teams. Examples are:

● asking fellow teams for information on what your team does that helps them, and what it should do differently to help them more

■ sending round a 'customer satisfaction' questionnaire on your team to other teams with which it interfaces

▲ inviting a very senior person in the organisation to discuss with your team his or her perceptions of how well it is supporting other teams.

Problem No. 4: conflict

Most of us dislike conflict – hence expressions such as 'Anything for a quiet life' and 'Don't rock the boat.' Yet teams are like families: they are places where people are brought more closely together, and where people are to some extent dependent on one another. So the risk of conflict is increased.

As you may remember from Chapter 1, some kinds of conflict can be just 'a stage the team is going through'. If it is a question of tussling for clarity, struggling to establish a team way of doing things, then this is not necessarily destructive. (But current thinking holds that there doesn't *have* to be conflict in a team before you get good teamworking – so don't go looking for it!)

How can you tell if conflict in the team is a problem rather than a developmental stage? If any of the following statements are true, then the conflict your team is experiencing *is* a problem:

● The conflict is repetitive.

■ It hurts people.

▲ It doesn't solve anything.

- It may have a personal or bitter quality to it.

- You feel ashamed of it.

- People leave the team because of it.

What can you do about conflict of this kind?

- Introduce more structure to teamwork in order to protect people. Conflict is most likely to rage in an open space. Run meetings tightly. Clarify roles and responsibilities. Draw boundaries between people, tasks, and events.

- Ask a skilled 'outsider' to work with the team for a limited period specifically to resolve the conflict. I was asked recently, for example, to run a day with an IT sales team that was being ruined by conflict largely based on a history of personal affronts between one individual and the rest of the team. The team needed to have the issues out in the open once and for all, so that they could move on to doing things differently in the future.

Problem No. 5: personality clashes

Sometimes two team members dislike each other intensely, cannot communicate without irritating each other, or need completely different team environments in which to work. One needs structure, the other spontaneity. One thrives on noise and debate, the other on plenty of reflection. Yet these two individuals are needed as part of the same team.

The first thing you as team leader must do is to check that it isn't either a conflict of interest or historical conflict that is causing the problem. If either is the case, then deal with it as I have suggested under Problem No. 4. If instead it is the kind of temperamental incompatibility we have just described, then try to:

- talk to each individual separately about the problem, outside the context of the team, and see what ways forward they suggest

- define their roles and responsibilities as clearly and separately as possible

- make sure they can maintain distance from each other in a way that doesn't disrupt the team; take simple practical steps, such as making sure their desks are not too close together or that team social events are not of a kind that forces intimacy.

There are few team objectives that can be achieved only if everyone likes one another. The 'softly softly' approach I am suggesting will allow mutual respect to grow, even when personal friendship is out of the question.

Problem No. 6: destructive communication patterns

Teams are like families in more ways than those we described earlier in this chapter: they get into bad habits. One particularly bad habit they're prone to is destructive communication patterns. Here are some examples:

- **The Put-down:**
  – intended to humiliate

  'That sort of unrealistic suggestion is typical of you, Jeff.'
  'You must be joking!'

- **The Wind-up:**
  – intended to heighten anxiety

  'There's talk of redundancies if your group doesn't win the orders we need…'
  'I wouldn't like to be in your shoes.'
  'Bit of a cock-up, eh?'

- **The Cynical Aside:**
  – intended to avoid responsibility

  'We've seen all that before.'
  'Damned if you do, damned if you don't!'

- **The Nit-picker:**
  – intended to assert superiority

  'I don't think you mean what you just said…'
  'You mean "and", not "but"!'

These kinds of destructive communication patterns can be indulged in through tone of voice as well as through words. And every team will have its own favourite set.

It's my experience that teams can identify their own set, and have quite a lot of fun policing themselves and eliminating them. Often all it takes is for someone to point out how much time and energy such communication patterns waste, and how they get in the way of constructive and creative communication.

Problem No. 7: groupthink

These are the symptoms of groupthink:

- little or no debate about issues

- little or no challenging of a decision, once made

- little or no self-criticism

- lots of self-congratulation

- defensiveness against criticism or challenge

- a sense of 'us against the world'

- an absolute conviction that the team is right

- declining interest in facts or opinions from outside the team.

Groupthink is dangerous to a team's and an organisation's well-being because it undermines the effectiveness of their decision-making. And it is widespread. The tighter-knit the team, the greater the risk of groupthink.

The best solution is an external force with impact and credibility to challenge the group. Some teams use external consultants; others keep their leader at some distance from much of the team's activity (so that he or she will not be sucked into groupthink); and yet others get people outside the team to review their work.

Problem No. 8: team nostalgia

The symptoms of team nostalgia are comments like this:

The best team I ever belonged to was on Project X. If you want to know what a real team looks like, you should have seen us on the Project X design team!

The answer to team nostalgia is prevention rather than cure. When a team's job, and hence the team, comes to an end, there are steps you can take to ensure the members join new teams with enthusiasm rather than regret:

- Formally review and acknowledge the team's achievements. Such a review is particularly powerful if it's led or contributed to by one of the team's important 'customers'.

- At the final team meeting, provide an opportunity for team members to say what they have valued about one another and what they will miss.

3 is there an ideal leadership style?

Are leaders born or made?

> 'She's a natural leader.'
> 'He's just not leadership material.'

How often have you heard comments like these? The view that some people are simply born with indefinable 'leadership qualities' is widely held. It contributes to the anxiety many of us feel when we are asked to lead a team at work. How do we know if we've got 'it'? What shall we do if we haven't?

It may be that to lead nations, religious movements, or armies some special innate gift is required. That is beyond the scope of this book. In my experience of ordinary teams at work, however, most people can make good leaders, given the right support and development.

What makes a good team leader?

The most useful way to think about the qualities and characteristics required of a good team leader is in terms of the main responsibilities he or she has. Although I shall identify for each responsibility a personality characteristic that equips someone particularly well for that responsibility, I do not mean to imply that certain personality types inevitably make good leaders and others inevitably make bad ones. Although personality is difficult or impossible to change, behaviour is not. Many of the most effective team leaders whom I have met have consciously modified their behaviour to do their job better. One team I worked with was, for example, led by the most extreme introvert I have ever come across. Despite this, he learned how to chair meetings effectively and get discussion going. In fact, his natural tendency to quiet observation and listening was a strength rather than a weakness in his leadership role.

> The team leader is responsible for organising the team to meet its goal(s).

To meet this responsibility, the leader needs a *structured approach* and good *planning ability*.

> The team leader is responsible for the quality of the team's output.

'The buck stops here.' To make sure that what the team is producing is good enough and achieved quickly enough, the leader must measure the team's effectiveness and give the team feedback. He must also look for and respond to feedback himself – from the team members, 'customers' of the team, and other teams with which his own interfaces. It helps if he has enough *self-confidence* to learn from mistakes and shortcomings along with *resilience* so that he doesn't give up when people criticise him or his team.

> The team leader is responsible for developing his or her team.

As the team develops it will require different things from its leader. At the beginning of its work, for example, it will benefit from lots of explanation and close supervision. When it is 'mature' it will work better if the leader steps back. To help the team move through the stages of development as smoothly as possible the team leader needs *flexibility*. If he or she is rigid about the way things are run, then the team will have nowhere to go.

> The team leader is responsible for the interface between his team and the organisation.

Teams have a natural tendency to become inward-looking, to focus on themselves and their own work, and to ignore or even compete with the rest of the organisation. The leader has a particular responsibility to make sure this does not happen to extremes, and to keep in mind the broader goals within whose context the team must achieve its particular goals. So he or she needs what is called in some of the organisations I work with *helicopter ability*, a combination of breadth of view and detachment. (If you're interested in a much more detailed analysis of how to combine organisational objectives with team objectives, and of what happens when you don't combine them, you can find one in *Pulling Together: Teamwork in practice*; see page 19.)

Is there an ideal leadership style?

The ideal leadership style is whichever works best for the team. The most effective team leaders either just happen to have a natural style that is right for the team they are working with at the time, or they are able to modify their natural style to suit different teams, or one team at different stages.

The important thing for a team leader is to know what his or her natural style is, and what other styles might work better: alert to his or her strengths and weaknesses, he or she will be able to change behaviour accordingly. So below we summarise four of the commonest styles, with the main characteristics of each. You might like to identify which style comes most naturally to you.

The directive style: useful for teams at start-up, or where the members have a lot to learn about the task.

- Leader has high level of interaction with the team.

- Most communication from leader is giving information and directions.

- Leader chairs meetings, allocates work, is the main source of feedback for the team.

- Team members respect and rely on leader.

The delegating style: useful for very competent, experienced teams.

- Leader has low level of interaction with the team.

- Most communication from leader is responding to proposals and suggestions from the team.

▲ Team members chair meetings, allocate work, give one another feedback and seek feedback directly from outside the team.

- Team members feel respected by leader.

The supportive style: useful for depressed, unsure teams, particularly those operating in an organisation hostile to, or critical of, them; most appropriate when the team is also reasonably competent.

- Leader has high level of interaction with the team.

- Most communication from leader is positive feedback and emotional support; leader will protect team from attack, and personally take the brunt of the organisation's criticisms.

▲ Team members chair meetings and so on, although leader may take on these functions if others are too busy or pressured.

- Team members trust leader.

The inspirational/charismatic style: useful for competent teams in situations of high risk.

- Leader's level of interaction with the team is highly variable – leader may 'walk the floor' or be more distant.

- Most communication from leader is visionary, motivational, and broad brush; leader represents the team in the organisation, and has high personal credibility and impact.

- Leader may or may not chair meetings and so on; tends not to get involved in the detail of tasks.

- Team members admire leader.

What is a team 'coach'?

A team coach is someone outside the team who has responsibility to develop the team to be more effective. The coach is concerned solely with the team's process, with how it operates, not with its task or its output, except in so far as these are relevant to its process.

Typically, a team coach:

- attends team meetings and helps the team review them

- supports the team leader by giving help to develop his or her style; discussing particular difficulties he or she has in leading the team; offering perspectives and perceptions on the team's strengths and weaknesses; identifying resources he or she can draw on to be more effective (techniques and approaches, visual aids, colleagues, courses, and so on)

▲ talks to the team's 'customers' (see Chapter Two) and either ensures they give feedback to the team or does so on their behalf

● encourages team members to monitor their own effectiveness and helps them plan how to do so

● networks with other team coaches, and keeps the organisation up to date on how well its teamworking overall is meeting its purposes, and on what else needs to change.

Very few teams need – or could justify the expense of – a full-time coach. So coaches are more usually people who have other jobs to do as well. Because of a particular aptitude for and interest in teamworking they do some team coaching for one or more teams maybe for a few hours a week. For the rest of the time, they are engineers, trainers, lawyers, managers... whatever. And no doubt they belong to teams themselves.

Six key skills for team leaders and coaches

Team leaders and team coaches have overlapping roles. And in many teams the team leader doubles up as coach. (Where it's particularly useful to have a separate coach is where the leader needs a high level of personal support.)

If you want to improve your performance either as team leader or team coach, these are the key skills you need to develop:

● sensitivity to people's unspoken fears, concerns and hopes

■ careful and accurate observation and listening

▲ ability to conduct reviews in a positive and constructive way

● coaching of individuals and the team in new ways of working

● support for individuals and the team at times of failure or difficulty

● help for team members to give one another feedback.

4 am I a natural team player?

What is the role of individuals in teams?

It's certainly true that some people find it easier to work in teams than others. People with a very individualistic approach which they find a great effort to communicate may prefer to see a task through from start to finish with a minimum of interaction. Very competitive people may find it hard to exchange personal goals for team ones. And extremely decisive thinkers will find it frustrating to discuss, debate, and work towards consensus.

But when people talk of 'natural team players' they usually have in mind the following qualities:

- willingness to share opportunity and credit
- ready communicator, open, direct
- likeability.

There are few individuals who can't demonstrate these qualities to some degree given the right team context, such as a team that is well led and has both clear goals and effective working methods, and fellow team members who are respected and trusted.

What is however more interesting than the crude distinction between 'natural team players' and the rest is the exploration of the differences between individuals in teams, of the variety of contributions that team members make, and of how very different styles can fit together to build a team that is more than the sum of its parts. So in this chapter there are two quizzes to help you explore what you yourself will naturally bring to a team, and to think about the different contributions your fellow team members make.

Thinking-style quiz

How people approach problems, how they make decisions, how they choose, weigh and use information – these are all components of 'thinking style'. Your thinking style will profoundly influence your contribution to team creativity and decision-making. You may also find that habitual conflict between yourself and another team member is in fact a result of different perspectives that you both take on issues. You can learn to capitalise on your own thinking strengths and to bridge the gap between yourself and fellow team members by identifying your own thinking style.

The quiz that follows is based on the famous psychiatrist Jung's theory of psychological types and on the 'Myers-Briggs Type Inventory'* which was developed from his theory. So the quiz looks at four questions about thinking style, which correspond to four important sources of differences between people:

- Am I an action-oriented thinker or a reflection-oriented thinker?

- Am I a facts-based thinker or an ideas-based thinker?

- Am I a logic-focused thinker or a values-focused thinker?

- Am I an ordered thinker or a spontaneous thinker?

To find out which of each pair you are, tick the statements listed that apply to you. Then, for each pair, count up the ticks. If you have many more 'action-oriented thinking' ticks than 'reflection-oriented thinking' ticks then it is clear you are naturally an action-oriented thinker. And so on. (Bear in mind you may not be strongly one way or the other for all four pairs.)

Once you have identified your strong thinking characteristics, read through all the statements for each pair of thinking styles again. Can you think of anyone in your team who is the opposite to you, for any pair? What do the statements tell you about his or her strengths in comparison with yours? How can you work together to get the strengths of both?

The quiz on pages 42–46 should help you appreciate why an effective team makes better decisions than a single individual: it has more perspectives and potential approaches available to it.

* The Myers-Briggs is available in the UK through: Oxford Psychologists Press, Lambourne House, 311–321 Banbury Road, Oxford, OX2 7JH. It is a full psychometric instrument and a licence is required to use it.

Action	Reflection
I enjoy meetings. ❏	I like to reflect thoroughly on an issue before saying what I think. ❏
I like to talk my ideas through with someone. ❏	I'm often quiet at meetings. ❏
I find I get energy and ideas from lots of discussion. ❏	Sometimes I get exhausted by having to explain things to people and listen to their views. ❏
I'm often one of the main contributors in a discussion. ❏	I tend to involve people in things I'm working on after I've done some thinking of my own. ❏
Other people usually know what I'm thinking. ❏	People quite often ask me how I came to my conclusions. ❏
Interruptions and changes of tack don't bother me. ❏	I think it's all too easy to rush into action without thinking things through. ❏
I'm often the first to state my opinion. ❏	I'm often the last to comment on an issue. ❏
Sometimes I worry that I've talked too much in a meeting. ❏	I sometimes feel people under-estimate the amount of thought I've put into a decision. ❏
I like to get other people's ideas and reactions to my ideas. ❏	I sometimes neglect to consult people. ❏
I think it's pointless to spend lots of time thinking without doing anything. ❏	I like to think that what I say is well thought through. ❏

Facts	Ideas
I'm known for taking a pragmatic approach. ❑	I'm known as an ideas person. ❑
I often remind people of the realities of a situation. ❑	I prefer to think about the big picture than about the details. ❑
I sometimes get impatient with airy-fairy ideas. ❑	People often comment on my enthusiasm. ❑
I think people often pay too little attention to the facts. ❑	I am good at creating patterns and links out of situations and facts. ❑
I'm often the one in a meeting who reminds others of important points of detail. ❑	I enjoy ideas and concepts. ❑
I get people to make explicit the steps in their logic. ❑	I believe it's often useful to forget all about the constraints and think 'blue sky'. ❑
I like to follow an argument through to the end to check it will work. ❑	I get frustrated by people who need everything spelled out. ❑
	I often think of new possibilities. ❑
I believe it's important to look at precedents and previous approaches which have worked. ❑	I'm sometimes caught out by matters of fact and detail. ❑
I think you can learn a lot from the past. ❑	I get bored with analysing the past and the present. ❑
I am more convinced by facts and logic than by inspirational talk. ❑	I think opportunities for positive change are often lost because of pessimists and nit-pickers. ❑

Logic		Values	
I can be very detached when it comes to making decisions.	❏	I naturally think of the human aspects of issues.	❏
People would say I was a logical thinker.	❏	I think heart and soul are just as important as logic.	❏
Sometimes I hurt people unintentionally when I'm simply trying to get to the right answer.	❏	My own value system often influences my approach to problems.	❏
I believe discussion, debate and challenges are necessary to test ideas and proposals.	❏	I feel uncomfortable when there is conflict and disharmony in groups to which I belong.	❏
I think it's more important to make a sound decision than to take people with you.	❏	I think the important thing in decision-making is to win people's commitment.	❏
When I'm under pressure I put the job first and can be tough with people.	❏	I believe getting people's trust is as important as being right.	❏
I think emotions get in the way of good decision-making.	❏	I am sensitive to other people's values and feelings.	❏
I don't generally allow my own values and personal feelings to influence decisions.	❏	When I am under pressure, a sense of harmony and belonging become even more important to me.	❏
I think the primary justification for doing something must lie in logical analysis of the pros and cons.	❏	I am good at building rapport with people without really trying.	❏

(continued opposite)

Logic (*continued*)

I would say that the more pressure I'm under, the more rational I become. ❏

Values (*continued*)

I consider mercy to be more essential than justice. ❏

Order

I'm often the one who organises agendas for meeting. ❏

I'm known for my good timekeeping. ❏

I think it's important to plan ahead and keep to the plan, unless one makes explicit provision for change. ❏

I get impatient with indecisive meetings. ❏

I make sure people are clear about who is to do what by when. ❏

I like advance notice so I can prepare properly. ❏

I think it's often more important just to make a decision than to make the 'right' decision. ❏

I am often the one who tries to move discussion forward to a conclusion. ❏

Spontaneity

I don't mind thinking on my feet – in fact, I quite enjoy it. ❏

I think it's important to keep an open mind for as long as possible. ❏

Sometimes I get so caught up in the discussion that I forget what we're meant to be deciding. ❏

I think a lot of problems are caused by overdecisiveness. ❏

Sometimes I feel as if I've been rushed into making my mind up. ❏

I am very responsive to new demands and new information. ❏

I get bored by predictability. ❏

Sometimes I procrastinate out of a sense that something may turn up which will change the whole picture. ❏

(continued on page 46)

Order (*continued*)		Spontaneity (*continued*)	
I work in a structured, methodical way.	❑	I enjoy the process of getting to a decision more than making the decision itself.	❑
Sometimes when I've made my mind up I refuse to enter any more debate on an issue.	❑	I am good at doing things at the last minute.	❑

Hopefully you now have some idea of what your thinking style is, and how it will lead you to be your most effective in a team. In the next chapter I shall introduce a team problem-solving framework that will help any team to make best use of the different thinking styles its members have.

Team-role quiz

The best-known model of individual differences in the team context is 'Belbin's Team Roles'. This model is based on study of the working habits of numerous teams, and covers more aspects than thinking style alone. It looks at social style, dominance and some emotional characteristics too.

There are nine team roles, according to Belbin's research. I have listed them below, with bullet-points underneath each one to describe it. If you tick those bullet-points that apply to you, you will get an idea of which role or roles you tend to take in your team. Ask yourself the same questions as you did for the thinking-style quiz to explore some of the roles your fellow team members take.

Belbin's team roles*

Implementer

- ⊙ stable and controlled – a practical organiser
- ▣ turns ideas into manageable tasks
- △ not easily deflated or discouraged
- ⊙ sudden change of plan may throw him/her
- ⊙ needs stable structures and tries to create them.

Resource Investigator

- ⊙ most immediately likeable – relaxed and sociable
- ▣ masses of outside contacts
- △ a salesman, diplomat and a liaison officer; can be mistaken for the 'ideas person', but lacks the personal originality that distinguishes the Plant (see overleaf)
- ⊙ preserves the team from stagnation and from losing touch with the outside world.

Co-ordinator

- ⊙ clarifies group's objectives and sets agenda
- ▣ stable, dominant, extrovert
- △ presides over and co-ordinates; not necessarily brilliant, and it is rare for many of the good ideas to emanate from him/her
- ⊙ is dominant but in a relaxed, non-aggressive way
- ⊙ social leader.

(continued on page 48)

---

* This table, whilst based closely on Belbin, contains material which our consultancy has developed to help people understand the roles, and for which Belbin is in no way responsible.

Shaper

- anxious, dominant, extrovert
- task leader; 'shapes' the team's efforts
- impulsive, impatient – easily frustrated
- quick to challenge and quick to respond to challenges
- sees team as an extension of his/her ego.

Plant or Creator

- high IQ
- scatters seeds which others nourish
- ideas person – originality and radical thinking
- most likely to start searching for original approaches
- may be bad at taking criticism of his/her ideas – may be offended and sulk.

Monitor–Evaluator

- high IQ; stable introvert in a balanced team
- serious, not exciting; measured, dispassionate analysis
- no original ideas but most likely to stop team from committing itself to a misguided project
- best skills: assimilating, interpreting and evaluating large volumes of complex written material
- can lower group's morale by being a damper at the wrong time.

Teamworker

- most sensitive of the team; most aware of individual needs and worries
- likeable, popular smoother – cement of the team
- loyal to team and builds on ideas
- good listener, communicates freely and encourages others
- does not like confrontation.

Finisher

- ○ anxious, introvert
- ▫ only at ease when has personally checked every detail
- △ maintains permanent sense of urgency
- ○ self-control; character impatient and intolerant of more casual members of the team
- ○ can be bogged down in detail and might worry the group.

Specialist

- ○ high degree of expertise in own field
- ▫ introvert
- △ narrowly focused on his/her own knowledge and/or skill base; not interested in people or in broader team issues
- ○ can be a bit of a 'law unto him-/herself'
- ○ adds significantly to the capability of the team.

How shall I fit?

Once you have identified the kind of contribution you will most naturally make in a team, you should ask yourself the following questions (thinking about these things will help you avoid limiting either yourself or the team):

◉ Am I unique in my team?

▪ How important is my approach to what the team needs to achieve?

▲ How much should I behave 'naturally', and how much should I restrain my natural style?

◉ Who am I most different from?

● How can I work effectively with him or her?

● Who am I most similar to?

■ How can I avoid forming a 'clique' with him or her?

▲ How would I like to develop personally through working with this team?

5 what do teams need to succeed?

In this chapter you will find a handful of tools and techniques for teams. I have chosen these particular ones because:

● they are simple

■ I have seen a variety of teams learn how to use them quickly

▲ teams have told me they improve their teamworking.

These tools and techniques help teams to develop a group method of working in which they have confidence.

Finally, I shall take a quick look at how the organisation for which a team works can support the team – if it chooses to! For a team to work well, it needs both the right internal processes and the right external context.

Tool One: the deceptively simple technique of 'brainstorming'

There are few working people now who haven't heard of 'brainstorming' – the generation of as many ideas as quickly as possible by a group of people. But many still don't realise its potential as a *team* tool.

Brainstorming rules are few and simple. If a team becomes skilled at working within them, it develops the capacity for the sort of 'clean communication' which is fundamental to effective teamworking. Also, participating in a good brainstorming session builds confidence and fun: there's nothing so motivating for a team as experiencing its own creative power. I was interviewing members of a new team in a US investment bank recently. When asked to recall what they had enjoyed about previous teams in which they had worked, 'good brainstorming sessions' were mentioned time and again. And because they encourage contributions from everyone, on an equal basis, these sessions build team unity, integrate part-timers and late-joiners, and include secretarial and administration staff in the decision-making processes of the teams they support.

Here is a quick reminder of the two basic brainstorming rules:

- Every idea is recorded: 'no idea is a bad idea'.
- No idea is evaluated.

What could be simpler? And yet sticking to these two simple rules is amazingly difficult. For this reason, when teams first start to run brainstorming sessions it's helpful for them to have a facilitator. This might be the team leader, the coach, or anyone in the team who is happy to take that role. The facilitator should not participate in generating ideas: his or her important function is to make sure that the two basic rules are kept to. He or she will also try to keep the energy of the team high in order to get everyone contributing and to encourage 'crazy' ideas, which are often the ones that lead to solutions.

In a good brainstorm, ideas will trigger other ideas and the flow of creativity will run around the team like an electric current. The key to this and to the teambuilding impact are those two simple rules. And 'no idea is evaluated' also means no groans, no raising of eyes to the ceiling, and no re-wording of ideas before they are recorded!

Even though in observation of hundreds of pseudo-brainstorms I have seen few that have really kept to the rules – ideas are criticised or selectively praised (often by the team leader), the scribe gets preoccupied with the wording, the team loses energy and commitment – it remains true that brainstorming is a tool of great untapped potential for many teams.

Tool Two: a structured problem-solving/decision-making process

There are many structured problem-solving processes, of varying degrees of complexity. It is more important, for effective teamwork, to use *a* structured process than to place a great deal of emphasis on *which* particular process to use. Most processes have the following stages, in some shape or form.

Stage One: define the problem

A great deal of team effort is wasted through different people in the team having different understandings of what the problem really is. It is particularly useful to ask everyone in turn to paraphrase the leader's statement of the problem. That way, misunderstandings and new perspectives are brought to everyone's attention.

Stage Two: present the background

In this stage, everyone should make available all the background information they have relevant to the problem. Much of this may well have been circulated before the problem-solving session. Of particular importance here are any constraints that limit the problem-solving process – for example, that the solution must be cheap or must be capable of immediate implementation.

Stage Three: generate ideas

This is the 'brainstorming' stage, where the brainstorming rules already described in this chapter should apply.

Stage Four: group ideas

This is best done by one or two of the team, and presented back to the whole team. It is essentially about turning the unstructured brainstorm into an ordered and coherent set of options.

Stage Five: choose the idea(s)

Now the task of the team is to evaluate the ideas logically, given all the background information, and select one or more ideas which they consider to be practical and effective solutions. Pros and cons for each idea should be stated. The process will be a combination of eliminating non-starters and highlighting promising solutions.

The benefit of this stage from a teambuilding point of view is that it provides a place for detached discussion during which team members come to understand more about one another's perspectives, expertise and reasoning style. It also encourages openness in argument, as well as argument about issues rather than personalities. To get these benefits, it needs (for all but the most mature teams) to be well chaired or facilitated.

Stage Six: check commitment

Once there is a shortlist of ideas, the team needs to set time aside to consider both how much commitment there is within the team to each idea and also how people outside the team are likely to react.

The benefits of Stage Six from a teambuilding point of view are that it encourages people to acknowledge feelings and helps prevent hidden agendas, which often have their roots in people's feelings.

Tool Three: action-planning

Nothing is more frustrating for teams than solving problems well but seeing nothing change. So they need to add the simple technique of 'action-planning' to their repertoire. The table below shows the format. A few basic rules govern its effective use:

● No one can be nominated for an action unless he or she agrees to take it on.

■ Actions must be described in precise, universally understood terminology.

▲ The team must agree that each action is worth doing.

Action-planning format

Overall objective:			
Action	By whom?	Completed by when?	Support/ resources required from team?

Tool Four: the PEP talk

As a tool for teams, PEP stands for 'Planning Effective Performance'. It consists of three simple questions, which teams should use frequently so that they gain in confidence and improve their effectiveness continuously:

- ● What did we do that worked well?

- ▣ What did we do that didn't work well?

- ▲ So what shall we do next time?

Unlike 'post-mortems', which focus on the past and encourage recrimination and despondency, the PEP talk assumes that the team will learn from all its achievements, failures and experiences how to be even more effective in the future. The PEP talk places as much emphasis on the positive as on the negative; and that balance of emphasis needs to be sustained by allocating equal time to each.

The PEP talk needn't take long. We have seen it used as effectively in a quick five minutes to review a meeting as in a two-hour review of a lengthy project.

Tools Six and Seven: flipcharts and 'talking walls'

I have found that it's hard to beat the simple flipchart as a practical tool to assist open and creative yet structured working.

The 'talking wall' is a physical space, never obscured, for displaying information about team members, team achievements, issues, intentions and queries. It is invaluable as a boost to internal communication. Not only that, if it's somewhere seen by people from other teams and kept 'reader friendly', it can help between-team communication too.

Even better is a team room, where all the wall-space can be used to display messages that are important to the team – to collect views, to report on where actions have got to and perhaps to put on show things the team is proud to have achieved.

How can an organisation guarantee a team will succeed?

In this book we have looked at what teams at work are and what they are for. We have identified common team problems and how to put them right. We have looked at team leaders, coaches and members. Hopefully you have a better idea of where you fit and what you can achieve in your team.

Let's finish with a quick look at the basics of what a team needs from its organisation (I have summarised them in the table opposite). If your team has all these basics, it is set for success.

The basics an organisation should do for its teams

An organisation should:

- ◉ give teams a clearly defined set of goals
- ▣ give teams a consistent message about what they are supposed to achieve
- △ base the reward system on team performance as well as individual performance (by 'reward system' I mean less tangible rewards such as praise, promotion prospects and the opportunity to wield influence, as well as money)
- ◉ give the team feedback on how well it is doing – all the time, honestly and positively
- ◉ take into account the impact on team functioning before it starts moving people around
- ◉ make sure the most senior team – such as the board or the management team – sets a good example of teamworking
- ▣ give teams the resources they reasonably request to achieve their goals
- △ support team leaders.

---

further reading

If you would like to read more about the topics covered here, the following books would be a good place to start.

BELBIN R. M. *Management Teams: Why they succeed or fail*. London, Heinemann, 1981.
— *Team Roles at Work*. Oxford, Butterworth-Heinemann, 1993.

HARDINGHAM A. *and* ROYAL J. *Pulling Together: Teamwork in practice*. London, Institute of Personnel and Development, 1994.

KATZENBACH J. R. *and* SMITH D. K. *The Wisdom of Teams: Creating the high-performance organisation*. Boston MA, Harvard Business School Press, 1993.

KROEGER O. *and* THUSEN J. M. *Type Talk at Work*. New York NY, Delacorte Press, 1992.

SENGE P. *The Fifth Discipline: The art and practice of the learning organisation*. London, Century Business, 1992.

WOODCOCK M. *Team Development Manual*. Farnborough, Gower, 1979.

With over 105,000 members, the **Chartered Institute of Personnel and Development** is the largest organisation in Europe dealing with the management and development of people. The CIPD operates its own publishing unit, producing books and research reports for human resource practitioners, students, and general managers charged with people management responsibilities.

Currently there are over 160 titles covering the full range of personnel and development issues. The books have been commissioned from leading experts in the field and are packed with the latest information and guidance to best practice.

For free copies of the CIPD Books Catalogue, please contact the publishing department:

Tel.: 020 8263 3387
Fax: 020 8263 3850
E-mail: publish@cipd.co.uk
Web: www.cipd.co.uk/publications

Orders for books should be sent to:

Plymbridge Distributors
Estover
Plymouth
Devon
PL6 7PZ

(Credit card orders) Tel.: 01752 202 301
Fax: 01752 202 333

Other titles in the *Management Shapers* series

All titles are priced at £5.95 (£5.36 to CIPD members)

The Appraisal Discussion

Terry Gillen

Shows you how to make appraisal a productive and motivating experience for all levels of performer. It includes:

● assessing performance fairly and accurately

■ using feedback to improve performance

▲ handling reluctant appraisees and avoiding bias

● agreeing future objectives

● identifying development needs.

1998 96 pages   0 85292 751 7

Asking Questions

Ian MacKay

(Second Edition)

Will help you ask the 'right' questions, using the correct form
to elicit a useful response. All managers need to hone their
questioning skills, whether interviewing, appraising or simply
exchanging ideas. This book offers guidance and helpful
advice on:

- using various forms of open question – including probing,
  simple interrogative, opinion-seeking, hypothetical,
  extension and precision etc

- encouraging and drawing out speakers through
  supportive statements and interjections

- establishing specific facts through closed or 'direct'
  approaches

- avoiding counter-productive questions

- using questions in a training context.

1998 96 pages   0 85292 768 1

Assertiveness

Terry Gillen

Will help you feel naturally confident, enjoy the respect of others and easily establish productive working relationships, even with 'awkward' people. It covers:

- understanding why you behave as you do and, when that behaviour is counter-productive, knowing what to do about it

- understanding other people better

- keeping your emotions under control

- preventing others' bullying, flattering or manipulating you

- acquiring easy-to-learn techniques that you can use immediately

- developing your personal assertiveness strategy.

1998 96 pages   0 85292 769 X

Body Language at Work

Adrian Furnham

If we know how to send out the right body signals, we can open all sorts of doors for ourselves at work. If we get it wrong, those doors will be slammed in our faces. *Body Language at Work* explores how and why people communicate their attitudes, emotions and personalities in non-verbal ways.

The book examines:

- the nature and meaning of signals

- why some personalities are easy to read and others difficult

- what our appearance, clothes and mannerisms say about us

- how to detect office liars and fakes.

1999 96 pages   0 85292 771 1

Constructive Feedback

Roland and Frances Bee

Practical advice on when to give feedback, how best to give it, and how to receive and use feedback yourself. It includes:

- using feedback in coaching, training, and team motivation

- distinguishing between criticism and feedback

- 10 tools of giving constructive feedback

- dealing with challenging situations and people.

1998 96 pages   0 85292 752 5

The Disciplinary Interview

Alan Fowler

This book will ensure that you adopt the correct procedures, conduct productive interviews and manage the outcome with confidence. It includes:

- understanding the legal implications

- investigating the facts and presenting the management case

- probing the employee's case and diffusing conflict

- distinguishing between conduct and competence

- weighing up the alternatives to dismissal.

1998 96 pages   0 85292 753 3

Introducing NLP

Sue Knight

The management phenomenon of the decade, neuro-linguistic programming (NLP) provides the techniques for personal growth. Use it to develop your credibility potential and value while also learning to excel at communication and interpersonal skills.

The author looks at:

● the essence of NLP and how it can work for you

■ using NLP to achieve what you really want

▲ how to build quality relationships and enhance your influence in the workplace.

1999 96 pages   0 85292 772 X

Leadership Skills

John Adair

Leadership Skills will give you confidence, guidance and inspiration as you journey from being an effective manager to becoming a leader of excellence. Acknowledged as a world authority on leadership, Adair offers stimulating insights on:

- recognising and developing your leadership qualities

- acquiring the personal authority to give positive direction and the flexibility to embrace change

- acting on the key interacting needs – to achieve your task, build your team and develop its members

- transforming such core leadership functions such as planning, communicating and motivating into practical skills that you can master.

1998 96 pages   0 85292 764 9

Listening Skills

Ian MacKay
(Second Edition)

Improve your ability in this crucial management skill! Clear explanations will help you:

● recognise the inhibitors to listening

■ listen to what is really being said by analysing and evaluating the message

▲ interpret tone of voice and non-verbal signals.

1998 80 pages   0 85292 754 1

Making Meetings Work

Patrick Forsyth

Will maximise your time (both before and during meetings), clarify your aims, improve your own and others' performance and make the whole process rewarding and productive. The book is full of practical tips and advice on:

- ● drawing up objectives and setting realistic agendas

- ■ deciding the who, where, and when to meet

- ▲ chairing effectively – encouraging discussion, creativity and sound decision-making

- ● sharpening your skills of observation, listening and questioning to get your points across

- ● dealing with problem participants

- ● handling the follow-up – turning decisions into action.

1998 96 pages   0 85292 765 7

Motivating People

Iain Maitland

Will help you maximise individual and team skills to achieve personal, departmental and, above all, organisational goals. It provides practical insights into:

- becoming a better leader and co-ordinating winning teams

- identifying, setting and communicating achievable targets

- empowering others through simple job improvement techniques

- encouraging self-development, defining training needs and providing helpful assessment

- ensuring that pay and workplace conditions make a positive contribution to satisfaction and commitment.

1998 96 pages   0 85292 766 5